Thomas Alva Edison

GREAT INVENTOR

How else could he find out how birds fly or what makes rain turn into snow? How else could he learn how steam engines and locomotives work? And telegraph machines? And sawmills?

It was true that things frequently went wrong when Al was playing and exploring. Ma Edison could not always keep an eye on him. She had so much work to do — cooking, cleaning, tending the fire, weaving cloth, and sewing. Even making candles.

Al had two sisters and a brother, but they were much older than Al. His sister Marion was married and gone. His other sister, Harriet Ann, and his brother, William Pitt, paid him little attention, so Al was often left to wander and play by himself.

Their village of Milan, Ohio, had wonderful places for a five-year-old boy to poke around. Besides the grain elevators, there was the lumberyard and the flour mill. There was also the canal with its boats pulled by teams of horses.

Of course, Al didn't mean to tumble down the grain elevator. Another time he didn't mean to fall into the canal while he was watching boats. He was just curious.

Al's pa still called him a troublemaker. Although his ma adored him, she admitted that her son was full of mischief. Neighbors whispered that little Thomas Alva Edison was an odd child.

Now and then Al was whipped with a birch rod for his misdeeds. His ma and pa hoped to teach him lessons in good behavior.

Al took his punishments bravely, but they did not stop him from poking around. They did not stop his curiosity.

One day when Al was six he went into his family's barn. There were no animals inside. Al lit a small fire "just to see what it would do." Flames leaped up and spread quickly. The barn was ablaze. Al escaped just in time, but the barn burned to the ground.

Al's pa shouted with anger. Fire was serious and dangerous. Al could have died! The whole village could have been destroyed!

Al was sorry about what had happened. But Al's whipping was harsh. When would Al ever learn to behave? Pa asked.

Samuel and Nancy Elliot Edison never knew what their son was going to do next.

2
A New Town

Pa Edison ran a lumberyard business in Milan. But his business began to fail. Al's pa decided to sell the house and move to a larger town.

Al was seven years old.

The family packed their belongings and headed north. They traveled by carriage, railroad, and steamboat.

At last they arrived at Port Huron, Michigan. The town was built on a spot where the river entered Lake Huron.

Ships traveled these waterways, bringing goods that people needed to live and work. Soon a railroad would be built and would run through Port

Huron. Railway cars would carry more goods to be bought and sold.

"Business will be booming here," Al's pa told the family. He began selling lumber and grain. And he talked about his dream — becoming rich someday.

The Edisons rented a large house near the lake and next to an army base. There was an army fort, a parade ground for marching soldiers, and a cemetery. There was a thicket of pine trees and a vegetable garden in the backyard. What wonderful places for Al to explore!

But not for long.

Soon after they arrived, Al became ill with scarlet fever. This illness was hard to treat. There was no medicine to fight it.

Day after day Al lay in bed. His fever continued to rise. He grew worse and worse. In the dark of the night he imagined ghosts in the cemetery and wolves in the woods.

Al's ma feared he might die. She stayed at his bedside from morning until night.

Then, luckily, Al began to recover. He felt strong again.

But he was left slightly deaf. Some doctors believe the deafness was caused by the high fever of his illness.

Al did not let this bother him much. Soon he started asking when he could go to school. Al was eager to learn.

Ma Edison worried that Al might become ill again. So she kept him home all year.

3
School Days

At last Al was allowed to start school. He could hardly wait. He ran to the one-room schoolhouse. He sat down with the other pupils.

The schoolmaster was Mr. Crawford. He wore a long coat and carried a heavy cane.

Al started to ask questions. "What is electricity . . . ? What . . . ?"

"Silence!" the schoolmaster cried. *Whack!* He smacked his cane on Al's desk.

Al blinked and slid down in his seat.

"Do not speak until I give permission," the schoolmaster said sternly. "Do you understand?"

"Yes, sir," said Al. His voice trembled.

The schoolmaster made the class sit still. Then he made everyone recite the alphabet. After that the pupils recited their arithmetic sums.

Once, when a boy made a mistake, the schoolmaster smacked his cane on the boy's knuckles.

School was not what Al thought it would be. How could he keep his knees from shaking with fear? he asked himself. How could he ever learn anything?

The same thing happened every day. Al got tired of memorizing lessons and reciting them over and over.

Even when Al finally had permission to ask questions, the schoolmaster hardly bothered to answer him.

One day Al raised his hand. "Please, sir," he asked. "Can you tell me: What is electricity? What are electric currents? How do batteries work?"

The schoolmaster flew into a rage. "Questions! Questions! I have no time to answer such questions!" he shouted at Al.

He called Al a backward boy with an "addled" mind. "Thomas Alva Edison will never learn anything," he said.

Al was hurt and angry. It wasn't fair! He ran home and told his ma what had happened. When she heard, she went right to the school.

"Al is not backward or addled," she told the schoolmaster. "He will never attend this school again!"

How glad Al was to hear that. But now how would he learn anything?

Al's sisters were much older than he. When he was eight, his sister Harriet Ann was twenty-two.

4
Lessons at Home

Al's ma decided to give him lessons at home. She had been a schoolteacher before she got married.

Ma Edison read to Al every day. He became a good reader. He didn't take much to arithmetic or spelling. But he liked history and literature.

One day his ma gave him a new book. It was called *Natural and Experimental Philosophy*.

The book was full of information about science. All kinds of science — such as electricity, magnetism, optics, and astronomy. It also explained how to make science experiments at home.

Al began "making things and testing things" for himself. There was nothing he liked doing better.

He set up a laboratory in his bedroom and collected materials — wires, batteries, magnets, scraps of metal, mercury, beeswax, feathers, chemicals, and powders. He needed plenty of bottles and jars, too.

When he couldn't find materials, he spent his pennies to buy them at the pharmacy.

Al earned money by weeding and hoeing the vegetable garden in the backyard. Sometimes his pa made him cart onions, corn, radishes, and beets around town to sell them. Al was glad to have the pennies, but he didn't like this work.

He only wanted to "make things and test things." His laboratory grew. Materials piled up everywhere. Chemicals spilled on the furniture and the floor. Sometimes an experiment exploded.

"He will blow us all up!" Al's pa cried.

Ma Edison convinced Pa to let Al keep the laboratory. "Let him be," she sighed. "The boy knows what he wants to do."

But she ordered Al to move the laboratory to the cellar. There Al lined up his bottles and jars again. He didn't want anyone to touch them. So he put a label marked POISON on each one.

Al spent many hours a day reading and experimenting. Soon he became interested in a new machine that was being installed in railroad stations — a telegraph.

The telegraph machine changed Al's life.

The telegraph sent and received messages through wires by bursts of electricity.

The sending operator pressed a key that moved up and down to send an electric pulse signal. A short press made a "dot." A longer press made a "dash." Dots and dashes were code signals for letters and numbers.

The receiving operator used a device called a "sounder," which caused an electromagnet to attract an iron bar. When the bar struck the electromagnet, it caused a sharp instrument to click the dots and dashes onto a strip of paper. The receiver could then decode, or "read," the message.

Al decided to make a small telegraph set. It

would take two machines and two people — a sender and a receiver.

Al got a neighbor named Jim Clancy to help. They read instructions in a book and got the materials they needed.

The boys fitted the materials into two small boxes. One box went into each boy's house. Then they attached wires to the boxes.

Next they strung the wires through the woods from house to house. They pegged the wires along nails driven into trees to hold the wires off the ground.

They tapped a few code signals back and forth to each other. Their telegraph set worked!

Of course, it was not like the telegraphs that railroad operators used. But Al and Jim had done a good job for beginners.

Al continued reading and experimenting at home. But when he turned eleven, the family decided to enroll Al in another school.

He had just suffered a bad ear infection. That made his poor hearing worse. As a result, Al couldn't hear very well inside the classroom. Also, there weren't enough books for everyone.

Outside, Al was awkward at sports and games. Children teased him and made him feel awful.

After a few months Al quit. He returned to his lessons and laboratory at home.

5
Working on the Railroad

The year was 1859. Pa Edison's dream of becoming rich did not come true. He ran into one business problem after another.

Port Huron had a new railroad — the Grand Trunk line. It connected the town to the busy city of Detroit, sixty-three miles away.

The railroad company put out a public notice: BOYS FOR HIRE. The company wanted boys to work as news and candy *butchers*. They would sell newspapers, cigars, sweets, and fruit to the passengers in the railway cars.

That's just what Al wanted to do! After all, he was already twelve years old. If Al could get a job, he could help earn money. He would be able to use some of the money for books and experiments.

"A job would be good for Al," said Pa. "It might keep him out of trouble."

Al's ma didn't like the idea. She worried about train wrecks. She worried about her son alone in a big city, where thieves and rough men roamed.

"Twelve is too young," she told Al.

"Lots of children work to help their families," Al argued. "I'll give you and Pa some of my earnings every week."

"What about your lessons?" she asked.

"I'll go to a free reading room every afternoon before catching the train back," Al said.

At last his ma agreed.

Al went to work for the Grand Trunk railroad. Each morning he boarded the train at seven o'clock.

He carried wares in a basket. Up and down the aisles of the cars he went, calling out, "Candy for sale! Peanuts, popped-corn balls, berries, and figs!"

The train moved along at thirty miles per hour. New customers got on at every station.

Al did well selling his wares. His pocket jingled with coins.

After four hours the train arrived in Detroit. Al kept his promise and went to the free reading room

Every day after Al worked as a newsboy on the Grand Trunk Railroad, he went to the Detroit Public Library where he attempted to read every book.

at the Young Men's Society. There were shelves and shelves of books!

Al tried to read the whole library. He started to read every book in order. But some were dull. Finally he chose only the ones he liked.

In the late afternoons Al boarded the train again. On the way home he sold bundles of newspapers. He had bought them at the office of the *Detroit Free Press*. "Read the latest news!" he called out. The passengers were good customers.

Al worked every day except Sunday. Week after week. Month after month. He didn't get back to Port Huron until dark each night. Then from the train station he had to ride a horse-drawn cart through a scary cemetery in order to get home.

He liked working. He liked earning money. (And it was fun when the engineer let him ride in the locomotive.) But Al often felt tired and lonely.

The conductor, Mr. Stevenson, was kind to Al. He listened to the boy when he had time. When Al told him that he missed working on his experiments, the conductor tried to help.

"Half of the baggage car is empty," he said. "Why not keep the materials there?"

Little by little, Al moved his bottles, jars, test tubes, scraps, and chemicals onto the train. He had a traveling laboratory!

One night they were on the way home. On one

shelf there was a stick of phosphorus in a bottle. This chemical was supposed to be kept safe in water all the time. But the water had evaporated, and Al forgot to add more.

The phosphorus got exposed to the air. That meant danger. Sure enough, all of a sudden it caught fire. The bottle fell off the shelf. Flames spread quickly onto the wood floor.

The conductor appeared just in time. He managed to put out the fire before there was a disaster.

The conductor turned red with rage. At the next station he threw Al's whole laboratory off the train.

6
Newspaper Boy

Al was lucky. He did not lose his job. Mr. Stevenson was truly a kind friend.

But Al needed something to replace his laboratory. He was fifteen now, and he wanted more to do during his hours aboard the train.

Finally, he had an idea. When he went to pick up his bundles of newspapers at the office of the *Detroit Free Press*, he often watched the printers set type and print the newspaper.

Why not print a little newspaper of his own, he thought. With money he had saved, he bought a small, used hand-printing press.

He also bought some old type — small metal blocks with letters and numbers engraved on them. He put all the equipment into the empty space of the baggage car.

Al taught himself to set type — letter by letter, line by line. He learned how to ink it and press paper over the wet type.

It was slow work, and it took lots of patience. But Al did it! He wrote and published a one-page newspaper. He called it the *Weekly Herald*. It was full of local news.

RIDGEWAY STATION

A daily Stage leaves the above named Station on St. Clair every day. Fare 75 cents.

CHANGE OF TIME

Express leaves Port Huron 7:05 PM.

LOST LOST LOST

A small parcel of Cloth was lost on the cars.

The finder will be liberally awarded.

BIRTH

At Detroit Junction G. T. R. Refreshment Rooms on the 29th inst, the wife of A. Little of a daughter.

MARKETS

Eggs, at 12 cents per doz.
Butter at 10 to 12 cents per lb.
Corn at 30 to 35 cents per bushel
Turkeys at 50 to 65 cents each

ADVERTISEMENTS

Splendid Portable Copying Presses For Sale at Mt. Clemens. Orders Taken by the news agent.

Al printed four hundred copies of the *Weekly Herald* and sold them all for two cents a piece. How proud he felt!

"Al Edison is a clever fellow," passengers said. "Are you going to become a newspaperman?" they asked him.

Al shook his head *no*. He liked working hard, but he didn't know what he wanted to do for his life's work.

Meanwhile, he found a way to make more money than his *Weekly Herald* was earning.

The year was 1862. The United States was in the midst of the Civil War. The North and the South were fighting bloody battles against each other.

One April day a huge battle was fought in the South at Shiloh, Tennessee. Thousands of soldiers were killed.

Al was still working as a news and candy butcher and printing his *Weekly Herald*. That April day he was visiting the *Detroit Free Press* to pick up newspapers to sell when news about Shiloh came in.

Al saw how interested the office people were when they heard the news. He realized that people everywhere wanted to know about the latest battle. At once Al saw the chance to sell more newspapers than ever that day.

He hurried to a man in charge of giving Al newspapers to sell.

"Would you trust me with a thousand copies?" Al asked. "I promise to pay back every cent."

"A thousand copies!" the man said. "What a crazy idea!" But he let Al take the newspapers on loan. Then Al got three friends to help him lug the newspapers to the train depot.

Suddenly Al had another idea. Why not get the news about the battle sent to the railroad stations right away? The operators could then announce the news to the waiting passengers. That way they would be excited and curious to read about Shiloh by the time their train — and Al, the news butcher — arrived.

Al asked the Detroit station telegrapher to send out the Shiloh news announcement to all the railroad stations. The Detroit telegrapher agreed.

By the time Al reached each station, a big crowd was waiting to buy newspapers.

At the first station he sold each copy for ten cents. At the next station he raised the price to fifteen cents. By the time the train reached Port Huron, he sold the last copies for thirty-five cents each!

Al was a clever fellow all right!

That night, after great success in sales, a thought came to Al. "The telegraph notice did the trick," he said to himself. "The telegraph is just about the

24

best thing going. I want to become a telegraph operator."

At age fifteen, with this exciting new venture, Al also decided to change his name. He now preferred to call himself Tom. This is how he introduced himself to new people he met. Only his family and old friends still called him Al.

7
The Telegraph

One hot summer day Tom stood waiting on the Mount Clemens station platform. A freight train was switching boxcars in the railroad yard.

Suddenly a loaded boxcar, with no brakeman aboard, rolled off a side track. It rolled onto the main track, gathering speed all the way.

Tom looked up. The stationmaster's little son, Jimmy, was playing on the main track in the path of the runaway boxcar. The boxcar moved faster and faster.

Tom rushed to the child and jumped onto the track. He grabbed Jimmy and leaped off with him. They fell onto the gravel. The boxcar sped past. They were both safe!

Mr. MacKenzie ran out of the stationhouse. How grateful he was to Tom for rescuing his son!

He wanted to reward Tom, but he had little money to spare. Then he thought about Tom always asking how the telegraph worked.

"How would you like to have telegraph lessons?" Mr. MacKenzie asked Tom.

"Would I!" Tom cried.

Tom gave half of his newspaper-and-candy butcher job to another boy. Then every afternoon Tom got off the train at Mount Clemens to attend his lessons.

The Mount Clemens Railroad Station looked like this in Thomas Edison's day.

Mr. MacKenzie invited Tom to live with his family. Tom paid for his share of the food during his stay at the MacKenzie house.

Months passed. Tom learned Morse Code — the dot-and-dash code for letters named after the inventor of the telegraph, Samuel Morse.

Tom learned to use the key, clicking the dots and dashes of outgoing messages. He learned to "read" and record messages that were coming in.

Tom became a good telegrapher. It was time to look for a job.

His first job was at home in Port Huron. He was hired to operate a small telegraph station in a corner of Mr. Walker's jewelry-and-variety shop. Tom set up a cot in the back of the shop because he had to work days and nights.

The telegraph station was not very busy. So Tom found other things to do. He read copies of a magazine called *Scientific American*. He tinkered with Mr. Walker's watch repair instruments. (This made Mr. Walker angry.)

During this time the Civil War was still raging. Everywhere men were called to fight in the battles. With so many men away from home, plenty of jobs were available. Tom decided to leave this job and found another job easily. It was on the Grand Trunk line, but it was far away — in Ontario, Canada, at the Stratford Junction station.

The young telegrapher was nearly seventeen.

At the Ontario station Tom became the night operator and was instructed to send a signal to the train dispatching office every hour. This was to make sure that he stayed awake.

It was a bother to wake up every hour. So he made a device to solve the problem.

He built a little wheel with a notched rim and attached it to a clock. This set off his signal automatically every hour.

The dispatching office found out. Tom was scolded, but he was not fired.

Later something else happened. It was much worse.

One night Tom was supposed to signal a freight train that another train was coming in the opposite direction.

But Tom was unable to get the message out in time. Luckily, the engineers of both trains managed to stop them before there was a collision. Tom was so upset that he left Ontario and never went back. After that, Tom tramped from city to city, working one telegraph job after another.

He went to Adrian, Michigan; and Cincinnati, Ohio. He went to Indianapolis, Indiana; Louisville, Kentucky; Memphis, Tennessee; and New Orleans, Louisiana.

Tom never stayed long at one job. Sometimes

he quit, and sometimes he was fired. It was hard for him to keep away from trouble, arguments, or misadventure.

Tom Edison had been a curious boy. Now he was a curious and restless young man. He still wanted to be free to wander and explore. Tom liked using his imagination better than following rules.

He was also a careless spender. Tom spent most of his earnings on books and materials for experiments. He saved little money for food, clothing, and shelter. Many nights he slept on a cot in a crowded rented room, or even on a basement floor.

Once he arrived in a city during a snowstorm. All he wore was a shirt, wrinkled trousers, and a pair of old shoes. He had only fifty cents in his pocket (along with a mess of wires, magnets, scraps of metal, and small tools!). People called him an oddball or a "country hick."

Tom didn't always mind his "odd" way of life. He had plenty of telegrapher friends — like Ezra Gilliland and Milt Adams — who moved around, too. They kept in touch with each other by telegraph messages.

But those early years were especially hard for Tom. He started asking himself new questions about telegraphy. "Do I really like this work? Is this the kind of work I want to do for the rest of my life?"

His answers were *no*. He was bored sending and receiving messages.

Besides, the telegraph was still the same machine as when Samuel Morse had invented it many years earlier. The telegraph could be improved, Tom thought. It could work faster and better.

At that time only one message could travel through a wire. Tom was aware that some telegraphers and inventors were working on a *duplex*. That was a wiring system to allow two messages to travel at the same time.

So far the duplex was not successful. Most people thought it was impossible. But Tom believed it *was* possible. He began experimenting with a duplex, too.

Maybe he could spend all his time improving inventions, he thought. Maybe someday he could even *be* an inventor himself!

8
Young Inventor

All Tom could think about were inventions. Sometimes he was fired up with excitement. Other times he walked around with feelings of gloom.

Where will I get money for a workshop? he wondered. What will I use to live on?

One winter day Tom arrived in Montreal, Canada. As usual, he had only a few coins in his pocket.

Days later he received a message from his friend Milt Adams. Milt was living in Boston, Massachusetts.

"The Boston Western Union Telegraph Company has a good job open," the message said.

Now called Tom, Edison worked as a Western Union telegraph operator. He was soon to become a full-time inventor.

Tom needed money badly. He set out for Boston at once.

Tom took the Western Union job. He and Milt shared a small room.

Boston was an exciting city for Tom. All around him scientists, engineers, and inventors were working.

Here, the public library and many shops offered wonderful collections of books. Tom read as much as he could. He especially liked the newest books on electricity.

After working hours, Tom returned his attention to the telegraph duplex. His imagination was fired up again!

By the next year Tom made up his mind. "I want to invent full time," he told Milt.

Tom quit his telegraph job and started working in a large workshop owned by Charles Williams.

He was surrounded by men who were tinkering with all kinds of things — like optic glass materials, fire alarms, and, of course, telegraphs.

Tom didn't care that he had no paychecks coming in. He was an inventor now. That is all he wanted to be!

Of course, he needed money to get started. So he made a deal with a few rich Boston men. They loaned him money.

If the inventions were a success, Tom would give them back their money — and more!

One of Tom's first projects was the duplex telegraph. He made some progress, but not enough. He decided to return to it later.

Tom had another idea. It was an electric voting machine for city councilmen in Washington, D.C. At that time, the council voted on laws by voice, and it took a long time to go around the room. With Tom's electric voter, each councilman had only to push one button for *yes* or another for *no*. The messages were carried by electric current from each man's desk to a lighted board at the front of the room.

In 1868, at age 21, Thomas got his first patent — for his electric vote recorder. It worked fine — but it was not a success.

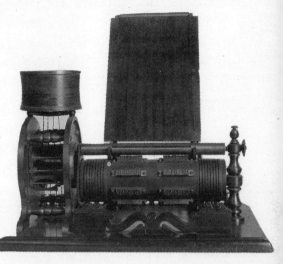

This was Tom's first real invention. He received his first patent for it. A patent is a legal grant given by the U.S. Patent Office. It protected his invention so no one else could steal his idea and make money from it.

It was a good invention, and it worked fine. But the councilmen didn't want it. They wanted to keep the old style of voting.

It was another gloomy time for Tom. But he didn't stay upset for long.

Tom made an important decision. From then on he would only make useful inventions that people wanted. Or else, surely he would starve to death.

He also decided to leave Boston and try his luck in New York City. There he went to work for a money investment business. The business used different machines that ticked out and printed stock investment prices on a ticker tape.

Soon Tom began to make improvements on the stock tickers and printers. The owners of the company were impressed and paid Tom well.

When he invented a new stock printer telegraph — "the gold printer" — Tom suddenly found himself a rich man! He was worth thousands of dollars!

At last he could start to fulfill his dream! He could have a workshop and laboratory of his own!

First, Tom sent some money to help his family in Port Huron. With the rest of his fortune, he moved from New York to the nearby state of New Jersey. In the city of Newark he rented one floor of a building. He installed equipment and hired two assistants.

By then he had spent most of his money. He hardly had saved a dollar. In fact, he didn't like bookkeeping or making budgets. His mind was too full of ideas and manufacturing matters to think about business details.

Tom didn't pay much attention to proper eating or sleeping, either. Often his dinner was only an apple dumpling and a cup of coffee at his desk. Or he simply forgot to eat at all!

Sometimes he went for long spells without sleep. Then he caught up on sleep a few hours at his desk or worktable. Once he used a big chemistry dictionary for a pillow!

He boasted that he didn't change his clothes until he was finished with a project. He didn't care about messy clothes or uncombed hair.

Tom worked on many inventions at the same time. Of course, he ran into plenty of problems. But he never gave up. Often he put something aside and went back to it later.

Little by little he made progress. He even met with success on the duplex.

In fact, he improved the telegraph system so much that now four messages could be sent at the same time! (Two from both ends of the wire.) This was called a *quadruplex*. How glad he was that he had not given up!

One day Tom met a sweet young woman. Her name was Mary Stilwell. Tom was shy with women, but he began talking to her. Soon he invited her out for a ride in his carriage.

Tom and Mary were married on Christmas Day in 1871. They had three children — one daughter, Marion Estelle, and two sons, Thomas Alva junior and William.

Mary Stilwell became the wife of Thomas Edison on Christmas Day, 1871.

Tom nicknamed Marion *Dot* and Thomas Alva junior, *Dash,* after the two telegraph signals.

Tom was glad to have a family. But he often spent more time at his laboratory than he spent at home. It was hard for Tom's family to live with a man who was so busy!

9
Invention Factory

The city of Newark was getting crowded. Tom began searching for another place to live and work.

Finally he settled on another area in New Jersey — Menlo Park. He bought several acres of land there and built a two-story wood building.

The building had a laboratory, a machine shop, a carpentry shop, an office, and a library. (It was surrounded by a picket fence to keep away cows that roamed in pastures nearby.)

People started calling the building an "Invention Factory."

This was the first research laboratory of its kind in the world. (It was one of Tom's inventions, too.)

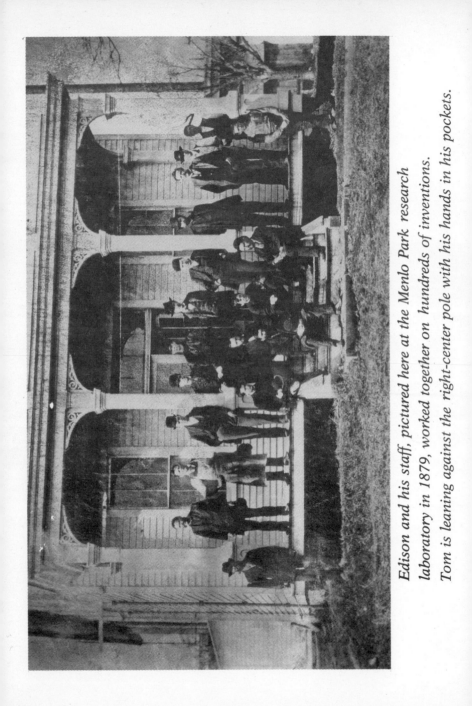

Edison and his staff, pictured here at the Menlo Park research laboratory in 1879, worked together on hundreds of inventions. Tom is leaning against the right-center pole with his hands in his pockets.

Tom hired many assistants — chemists, mathematicians, machinists, and draftsmen.

His chief assistant was an English engineer and draftsman named Charles Batchelor. Another important assistant was John Kreusi, a Swiss clockmaker.

Tom and his team wasted no time getting started.

One of the first inventions was an electric pen. Later, Tom used the electric pen to make stencils for a copying press. The pen punched holes into waxed paper in the shape of letters. A cylinder, soaked in ink, was rolled over the punctured waxed paper. The ink seeped through the holes onto another sheet of paper underneath. This made a printed duplicate copy of the wax paper original. So the waxed paper became a *stencil,* and many copies could be made.

Tom and his assistants developed and manufactured several products during the years following. The men were full of high spirits.

Of course, they were not the only inventors during the 1870s. There were dozens in the United States and across the globe.

One was a young man from Scotland who was living in Boston. He was born in 1847, the same year as Tom.

His name was Alexander Graham Bell. Alec, as

he was called, was a teacher of deaf pupils. His mother was deaf, and Alec was married to a deaf woman.

Alec was especially interested in sound and the communication of sound. He began thinking about inventing an instrument to convert human voice sounds into electrical current. A speaking telegraph!

He began his experiments at home. Then he moved them to the large Charles Williams workshop. That was the same place where Thomas Edison had started.

Alec spent long, hard hours with all kinds of equipment — such as tuning forks, wires, transmitters (instruments that send messages) and receivers (instruments that take in messages sent to them).

In time he developed an instrument with a transmitter and a receiver (the "mouth" part).

Alec had an assistant, Thomas A. Watson. Together they conducted one test after another to learn more about vibrations and sound waves.

One hot June day in 1875, Alec managed to hear a few voice sounds over the wire. The sounds were scratchy and faint, but it was an exciting moment!

Finally, a year later, after making improvements, Alec and Watson could hear actual words. The telephone was invented.

Alexander Graham Bell was granted a patent on his invention. Then he helped to form the Bell Telephone Company. It was a large company that hoped to make a fortune.

But Western Union wanted to make money in the telephone business, too.

So they hired Tom Edison to improve the telephone further.

Tom also had experimented with voice-carrying instruments. He was sure that he could find a way to make speech sound clearer than Bell's telephone did over the telephone wire.

In his factory Tom built several telephone models. He applied many materials to the receiver. He tried one kind after another — paper, sponges, swatches of felt, graphite, cork, whatever came to his mind.

Little by little he made progress. But he was not fully satisfied.

Then one night Tom was working late. His kerosene lamp went out. In the dark he stumbled to refill it with oil.

After he relit the light he noticed the inside of the kerosene lamp. It was thick with carbon black (soot). Why not try *this*? he thought. Anything was possible.

Tom scraped off some carbon black. Then he applied it to the disk in the receiver of one of his telephone models. The sounds of the voice came through louder and clearer than ever before. The carbon transmitter worked!

Tom made other improvements on the telephone, too. Western Union paid him well.

Thomas Edison made improvements to the telephone, which was invented by Alexander Graham Bell in 1876.

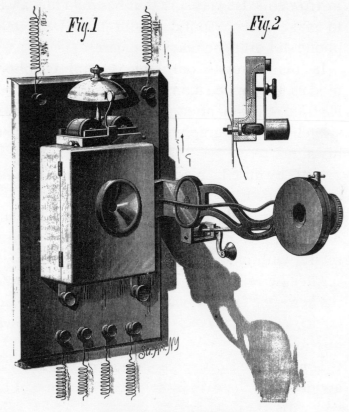

EDISON'S NEW TELEPHONE.

Soon Western Union and the Bell Telephone Company found themselves in the middle of a business "war." Finally they struck a deal.

Western Union agreed to move out of the telephone business and stay only with the telegraph. The Bell Company agreed to stay only with telephones and not compete with the telegraph company.

Tom still didn't like to bother with money details. Company "wars" were another kind of business he wasn't interested in getting involved with.

But the telephone itself continued to excite Tom.

He wrote hundreds of pages of notes on sending and receiving sound. He experimented again and again with sound waves making vibrations on the telephone diaphragm (a surface that vibrates when sound waves hit it).

Then an idea flashed through his mind. Why not record those vibrations? he thought. This was one of his best ideas yet!

10
The Talking Machine

Tom decided to invent a machine that would *record* voices and then *talk back,* replaying the voices just recorded.

Usually his assistants believed in his ideas. But this time they shook their heads and called the idea crazy.

Tom didn't mind. He wrote pages and pages of notes. Then he drew hundreds of sketches. Assistants set to work on the first model.

It was made with a brass cylinder covered with tinfoil.

The cylinder fitted over a shaft with a hand crank to turn it round and round.

The phonograph was Edison's first major invention.

Another piece in front of the cylinder had a mouthpiece and a little needle.

As the cylinder turned, the needle tip scratched grooves into the tinfoil.

When the model was finished, everyone in the laboratory gathered around. The assistants didn't expect much to happen.

Tom turned the hand crank to rotate the cylinder. He shouted into the mouthpiece:

"Mary had a little lamb/Its fleece was white as snow/And everywhere that Mary went/The lamb was sure to go."

Tom moved the shaft back and connected it to

47

a second needle on the other side. Then he turned the handle again.

Out came Tom's voice: "Mary had a little lamb . . ."

Amazing! Astonishing! The men could hardly believe it. (Tom was the most excited of all!)

December 6, 1877, was a time of wonder in the invention factory. Thomas Alva Edison had invented the phonograph.

Two months later he was granted a patent. Then he helped form the Edison Speaking Phonograph Company and began manufacturing the product.

News of the talking machine had spread everywhere. Newspaper reporters and magazine writers flocked to Menlo Park. Tourists came by the trainloads just to peer at the factory.

Tom was called the "Wizard of Menlo Park." But the word "wizard" didn't seem right. It meant magic, and Tom said there was nothing magical at Menlo Park. His inventions came from thinking and hard work!

Some people thought the phonograph was a clever invention. Others called it a "scientific toy." There were a few who thought it was just a trick. But everyone wanted to see how it worked.

Tom was invited to many cities to give demonstrations. In one city he recorded his voice reciting a poem and whistling a tune. In another city he recorded a man playing "Yankee Doodle" on a cornet.

How delighted people were with the talking machine! Tom had the best time of all!

One day an important group of scientists invited him to Washington, D.C., the nation's capital. Tom brought along his assistant, Charles Batchelor, to help show the new work. After their demonstration the scientists applauded loudly.

That night, President Rutherford B. Hayes heard that Edison was in town. It was very late, but he wanted to see and hear the talking machine. So he invited the inventor to the White House.

When Tom arrived, it was almost midnight. Mrs. Hayes was sleeping, but she was awakened and came downstairs.

The president was thrilled at the demonstration. And Tom had a merry time at the White House.

The talking machine became a big success! But still people thought it was only a charming toy.

Tom disagreed. He was sure that someday the phonograph would bring great music to people. It would preserve important speeches, he believed. And it would be useful in education.

Meanwhile, Tom had another idea to work on. A bright idea indeed!

By 1881, people could listen to music on the Edison phonograph.

11
The Electric Lamp

It was 1878. People used oil lamps, gas lights, or candles when they wanted to light their way in the dark.

For a long time scientists and inventors had worked on ways to create better and longer-lasting light.

So far they only had *arc* lighting — sparks of electricity that jumped across spaces between pieces of carbon (the substance at the end of a burnt matchstick).

But arc lights were little help. They lasted only a few hours. And arc lights could only be used outside. Their glow was blinding. And they smelled awful.

Tom was now thinking about improving light.

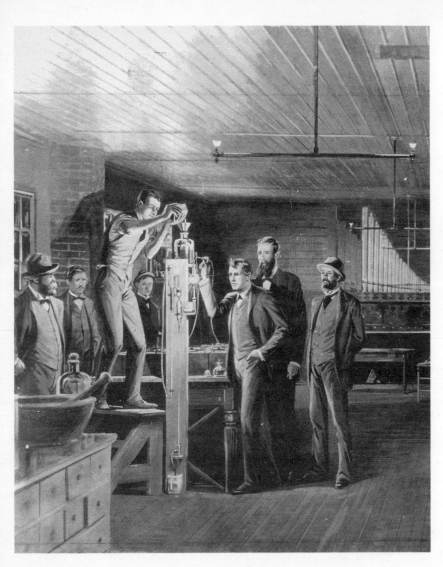

An artist shows Tom and his helpers at work in the lab. Many long, hard hours of experimenting with different materials led to one of the greatest inventions of all time.

His goal was to control *incandescence* (the bright glow from heat).

He filled hundreds of notebooks with ideas about how to invent a practical lamp. He drew pages and pages of sketches.

Tom wanted the lamp to be safe, long-lasting, and cheap to make. All together he considered about 3,000 ideas!

He decided on the most important parts that he needed: first, something to use as a *filament* (a thin fiber or wire); second, a glass with no air in it to seal around the filament.

Then an electric current would pass through a wire and heat the filament. And that would make a glow! A glow lamp!

"The electric lamp will be finished in six weeks," Tom announced.

Tom and his assistants worked long hours.

Six weeks passed. Then months. Sometimes Tom's eyes were so tired that they burned with pain.

It was hard to find the right material to use as a filament. The inventors tried one after another — wires, weeds, threads, metals, fish lines, wood splinters, bamboo, even a hair from a man's beard! (The beard belonged to Tom's old telegraph teacher, Mr. MacKenzie, who had come to work for him.)

Some of those filaments burned out quickly. Others melted, split apart, or flickered on and off.

There were questions about the glass, too. What shape should it be? What size? How could they get all the air out? (Oxygen in the air causes a lit filament to quickly burn up.)

More months passed. Money was running out. Again, people called Tom foolish. One magazine called him a "show-off."

Tom's assistants grew weary. But not Tom. "I do not ever feel discouraged," he said.

Finally they discovered how to get all the air out of the glass. They developed a special mercury vacuum pump to remove it.

Edison wrote many notes and sketched his ideas. These pages from his notebook show what he was working on in February 1880.

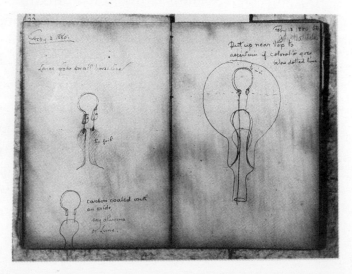

Then on October 22, 1879, Tom tried a new filament material — a cotton thread. He coated it with carbon.

An airless glass was ready. Tom sealed the coated thread inside.

Then he turned on the electric current. The filament glowed. When Tom turned up the current, it glowed brighter.

Everyone stared at it. Hours went by. The filament didn't burn out.

They waited and waited. The lamp continued to glow. It lasted thirteen and a half hours!

The next models glowed many more hours.

Thomas Alva Edison's electric lamp was a wonder! One New York newspaper announced:

EDISON'S LIGHT
THE GREAT INVENTOR'S TRIUMPH
IN ELECTRICAL ILLUMINATION
IT MAKES LIGHT WITHOUT GAS OR FLAME,
CHEAPER THAN OIL

Huge crowds boarded the trains to Menlo Park. They wanted to see the "light of the future."

Tom planned a big New Year's Eve surprise for the public. He strung rows of glow bulbs on trees

Edison lit up the world with his invention of the first lightbulb.

that lined the road near the train station.

When it grew dark, he pulled the switch. The entire road lit up brightly! What a wonderful sight! The guests could hardly believe their eyes!

Thomas Edison brought light into darkness. He created "daytime" in the middle of the night. He changed the world forever.

Tom was always practical. Now he wanted to bring light to large areas and then to entire cities.

He formed an electric light company. Many people helped to get it started by investing money.

Tom spent the next years developing a system to generate and send out electric power.

The system was so new that along the way Tom had to invent more than three hundred devices and machines to help make the system succeed.

There were generators, cables, switches, sockets, fuses, tubes, meters, and conductors.

The first power station — a main building that generates and controls electricity throughout the district — was built on Pearl Street in New York City. Tom hired a crew of two thousand people to help with the gigantic job. They (Tom, too) worked day and night digging ditches, installing pipes, and connecting wires.

There were plenty of breakdowns and delays, including sudden bursts of flame, called flash fires. But the workers pushed on.

Finally, one September afternoon three years later, in 1882, Tom pulled the main power station switch. Suddenly electric lights glowed throughout the district.

Soon other cities across the country were lit. And then cities across the globe.

Tom became a rich man, but he spent more money than he earned.

"No man can invent and do business at the same time," he said. "I always invent to obtain money to go on inventing."

12
Moving Pictures

Tom became famous all over the world. He met presidents, kings, and queens. But he didn't care much about fame. He continued to work as hard as ever.

He also worried about how to get money for new projects. And he worried about competition from other inventors and companies. Sometimes it is hard for inventors not to be jealous of one another.

Then one spring, Tom's wife Mary became ill. She grew worse and worse. At the end of the summer she died.

The Edisons had not had a happy marriage. Tom had not spent much time being a husband or father. But Tom had cared about Mary. Now he missed her.

He was left with three children. Marion was almost twelve. She went away to boarding school, but lived with Tom during vacations.

Thomas junior and Will were younger. They were sent to live with their grandmother and an aunt.

Two years later Tom met another young woman. Her name was Mina Miller.

Tom proposed marriage to her. Mina knew that it would be hard to live with a busy and famous

Mina Miller was the second wife of Thomas Edison.

man. But she loved Tom and agreed to marry him.

They moved to another town in New Jersey — West Orange. Thomas junior and Will came to live with them.

Tom and Mina had three children together — Madeleine, Charles, and Theodore.

In West Orange, Tom built a grand laboratory and factory. There he and his assistants worked on many projects at once.

For instance, he improved his phonograph, as well as another inventor's version of an electric battery. When X rays were discovered, he designed a fluoroscope screen to use for studying X-ray pictures.

There were also projects that failed. Tom couldn't find a substance in the United States for making rubber that was as good as a substance that came from certain trees in South America. Also, he could not get people interested in a new way to build concrete houses. People felt more comfortable building houses "the old way" instead of listening to new ideas.

There were other troubles for Tom, too. Once a pot of hot wax exploded in his face and seriously burned him. Then one winter evening a fire broke out in one of his factory buildings. Almost everything was destroyed. Only the laboratory was spared.

Days later Tom began borrowing money to re-build. Soon the factories were back in business.

Inventions. Inventions. Inventors and scientists everywhere were helping to change the world.

One new invention was the camera. People liked taking pictures.

Tom liked taking pictures, too. He also enjoyed studying the way cameras and film worked.

Soon Tom and several other people started getting new ideas about photography.

Pictures of people standing still were fine, they thought. But why not create a way to make pictures move? Moving pictures!

Tom and an assistant, William K. L. Dickson, created one of the first methods.

It was a "box" with a peephole, called a kineto-scope. Inside there was a loop of film on rollers, a light to shine through the film, and a motor to set it rolling. When the film was rolling, the pictures looked as if they were moving. One person at a time was able to look into the peephole.

One filmstrip showed a man juggling. Another showed two men in a boxing match.

Soon inventors and photographers everywhere were experimenting further.

One man developed a machine that could project large images onto a screen. Tom worked on a moving-picture projector like that, too.

Now people didn't have to look in a peephole one at a time anymore. Many viewers could enjoy moving-picture entertainment together.

The "movie business" was born.

Tom built the first movie studio in the world. The outside of the building was completely black. The walls inside the studio were painted all black, too. The studio roof was built to open up to let in sunlight. The sunlight on the performers contrasting with the blackness of the walls created the best way to film them.

People called the studio building ugly. But it did the job!

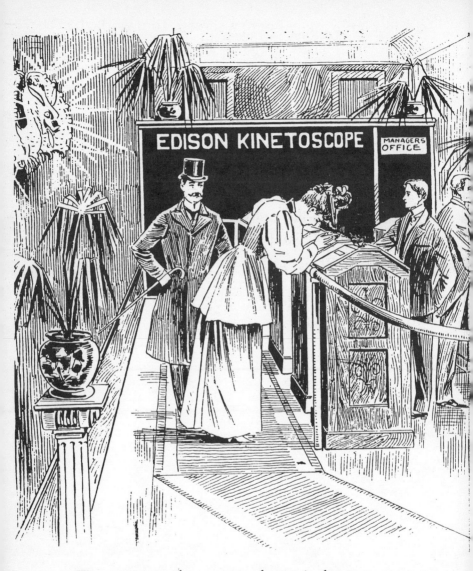

Kinetoscope parlors were early movie theaters.

The first one opened in New York City on April 14, 1894.

13
Celebration

The years passed. Thomas Edison suffered many illnesses. His hearing grew worse.

But he never stopped reading and learning. He never stopped thinking. He never stopped working.

When the United States entered World War I in Europe, the president asked Tom for help. Tom, who was seventy years old, agreed and created a research department for the U.S. Navy. He also worked on parts for submarines and devices to find enemy submarines.

Tom was praised and honored often.

In October 1929 the lightbulb was fifty years old. It was time for a big celebration. Tom was

Thomas Edison's eightieth birthday in 1927 was big news. Photographers from many papers came to his West Orange home to take his picture, along with his friend and fellow inventor Henry Ford (behind Edison).

A special "Golden Jubilee" emblem was created for the 50th anniversary of Edison's lightbulb.

invited to a special party at a museum in Dearborn, Michigan.

"Edison gave light to the world!" people cheered. And electric power, better transportation, improved communication, entertainment, comforts at home and at work. All together he was awarded 1,093 patents!

The celebration was exciting for Tom.

Afterward, Tom returned to West Orange. He and Mina lived there quietly for two years.

Tom's health failed rapidly. And then on October 18, 1931, the great inventor died at home.

People hailed him as the "man of the century" and "citizen of the world."

The life and work of Thomas Alva Edison was honored everywhere.

What would our world be like today if not for the inventions of Thomas Alva Edison?

From the Laboratory
of
Thomas A. Edison,

Orange. N.J. Aug 14 1918.

Dear Carty

In reply to your question, let me say that I was the first person to speak into the first phonograph. The first words spoken by me into the original model, and that were reproduced were "Mary had a little lamb" and the other three lines of that verse.

Yours sincerely

Thos A Edison

A handwritten note from Thomas Alva Edison to General John J. Carty is just one of the many Edison documents that were saved for all to see and learn from.

SCHOLASTIC BIOGRAPHY

❑ MP45877-9	Ann M. Martin: The Story of the Author of The Baby-sitters Club	$3.99
❑ MP44767-X	The First Woman Doctor	$3.99
❑ MP43628-7	Freedom Train: The Story of Harriet Tubman	$3.99
❑ MP42402-5	Harry Houdini: Master of Magic	$3.50
❑ MP42404-1	Helen Keller	$3.50
❑ MP44652-5	Helen Keller's Teacher	$3.99
❑ MP44818-8	Invincible Louisa	$3.50
❑ MP42395-9	Jesse Jackson: A Biography	$3.25
❑ MP43503-5	Jim Abbott: Against All Odds	$2.99
❑ MP41159-4	Lost Star: The Story of Amelia Earhart	$3.50
❑ MP44350-X	Louis Braille, The Boy Who Invented Books for the Blind	$3.50
❑ MP48109-6	Malcolm X: By Any Means Necessary	$4.50
❑ MP65174-9	Michael Jordan	$3.50
❑ MP44154-X	Nelson Mandela "No Easy Walk to Freedom"	$3.50
❑ MP42897-7	One More River to Cross: The Stories of Twelve Black Americans	$4.50
❑ MP43052-1	The Secret Soldier: The Story of Deborah Sampson	$2.99
❑ MP44691-6	Sojourner Truth: Ain't I a Woman?	$3.99
❑ MP42560-9	Stealing Home: A Story of Jackie Robinson	$3.99
❑ MP42403-3	The Story of Thomas Alva Edison, Inventor: The Wizard of Menlo Park	$3.50
❑ MP44212-0	Wanted Dead or Alive: The True Story of Harriet Tubman	$3.99
❑ MP42904-3	The Wright Brothers at Kitty Hawk	$3.99

Available wherever you buy books, or use this order form.
